A Wild Animal

Contents

Chapter 1
Good-bye

Dr. Butler watched the little fawn
trotting around the yard
after Goldie.
Goldie barked happily,
and the little fawn tossed his head
and did a small dance.

"I think it's time for us
to take the fawn
to someone who can help him
learn to live in the wild,"
said the veterinarian.

Kelsey and her dog Goldie
had been taking care
of the little fawn
ever since they had found him
under the porch of Kelsey's house.

"No!" said Kelsey. "No!
He's too little to live in the woods
by himself."

"He is growing up. You know that,"
said Kelsey's father.
"He needs more room.
He can't live in the house
with us!"

"We could make him a barn
or something," said Kelsey.
She pointed to the yard.
"We have a huge yard.
There's plenty of room!"

"But that wouldn't be fair to him.
He should be in the wild
with other deer,"
said Dr. Butler.
He put his hand on Kelsey's shoulder.
"I know how much
you love the fawn,
but you need to think about
what would be best for him!"

The next day, Dr. Butler
and his son Josh came over
with their van.
Kelsey and her dad
lifted the fawn
into the back of the van.
Josh and Kelsey sat in the back
with him.
"Can Goldie come? She will want
to say good-bye, too!"
said Kelsey.

"Sure," said Dr. Butler.

Kelsey's dad opened the door,
and Goldie jumped into the van.

"Goldie doesn't know
what's going on.
She thinks she is
the fawn's mother.
She is going to be very upset,"
Kelsey said to Josh.

Chapter 2
Getting Ready for the Wild

"This is Ms. Martin,"
Dr. Butler told Kelsey and her father.
"She has helped place
many wild animals
back into the wild."

Ms. Martin smiled at them and
turned to the fawn,
who was standing shyly
next to Goldie.
She said, "Well,
who do we have here?
This is one fine-looking animal!"
She scratched the fawn's ears.

Ms. Martin took them around
to the back of her house.
They sat on some lawn chairs
and looked out at the huge forest
that started at the edge
of Ms. Martin's property.

"I will be teaching the fawn
how to find food
and take care of himself,"
said Ms. Martin.
"There are some young deer
that live nearby. I am hoping they
will let the fawn join them."

"But what if they don't?"
asked Kelsey.

"Well, he will still learn to be
on his own. When he is an adult,
he will find a mate
and start his own family,"
Ms. Martin told her.

Kelsey knelt down and hugged
the fawn. "Good-bye, Baby,"
she whispered to the fawn.
"I will always remember you.
I hope you will remember me!"
She kissed the fawn's nose and
scratched his ears.

Goldie nuzzled at the fawn's neck.
She seemed to know
they were saying good-bye.
Kelsey's dad had to pull Goldie
to the van.

Several times, Kelsey's father drove
her over to Ms. Martin's
so she and Goldie
could see the fawn.
Each time he looked less like a baby.
"I wish he could live with me,"
she wept.

"I know, honey," said Ms. Martin.
"But it just wouldn't
be right for him."

"I'll never see him again!"
Kelsey cried.

"No, but you will remember him,"
said Ms. Martin.
"He will always be in your heart!"

Chapter 3
Home Again

School was out for the summer.
Kelsey and Josh were building
a tree fort.
Josh was whistling
as he hammered away.

Suddenly Goldie started yipping.
Her ears were up
and her tail was wagging wildly.

Kelsey climbed down
out of the tree.
"What is it, Goldie?"
Goldie raced towards
a clump of trees.
Kelsey ran after her.
She stopped in amazement.
"Baby!" she said. "It's Baby!"

Josh ran up.
"Hey!" he said. "It *is* Baby!"

There, looking back at them,
was the fawn.
Behind the fawn
were two young deer.
Goldie ran up to the fawn.
The two other deer turned and ran
into the woods, but Baby stood
and let Goldie run
around and around him.
He tipped his head
and tapped his hoof in the dirt.

"Look how big he is!" said Kelsey.
She walked slowly towards him.

"Hey there," she said softly.
"Did you come by to say hello?
You are so big and beautiful.
Goldie, our baby is growing up.
Look, he's a handsome deer!"
Goldie yipped and danced around.

Suddenly, Baby turned
and was gone.
Kelsey had never seen anything
as beautiful as her fawn
leaping through the trees
after his friends.

"He came back to see us, Goldie!
He'll visit us again!"
And now Kelsey knew her father
and Dr. Butler were right.
Baby needed to be free and to live
like other wild animals.
But he did remember them,
and had found his way home.
She knew he would come again!